ZOOM in 'on...

HOUSE
OF HORRORS

Richard Spilsbury

Enslow Publishers, Inc.
40 Industrial Road
Box 398
Berkeley Heights, NJ 07922
USA

http://www.enslow.com

This edition published by Enslow Publishers Inc.

Library of Congress Cataloging-in-Publication Data

Spilsbury, Richard, 1963-
  Zoom in on house of horrors / Richard Spilsbury.
      p. cm. –(Zoom in on–)
  Summary: "Get an up-close look at a variety of insects and creatures that live in our houses"–Provided by publisher.
  ISBN 978-0-7660-4312-1
  1. Household pests–Juvenile literature. I. Title. II. Series: Spilsbury, Richard, 1963- Zoom in on–
  TX325.S65 2013
  648'.7–dc23   2012045287

Future edition:
Paperback ISBN: 978-1-4644-0569-3

To Our Readers: We have done our best to make sure all Internet addresses in this book were active and appropriate when we went to press. However, the author and the publisher have no control over and assume no liability for the material available on those Internet sites or on other Web sites they may link to. Any comments or suggestions can be sent by e-mail to comments@enslow.com or to the address on the back cover.

Printed in China
122012 WKT, Shenzhen, Guangdong, China
10 9 8 7 6 5 4 3 2 1

First published in the UK in 2012 by Wayland

Commissioning editor: Victoria Brooker
Project editor: Kelly Davis
Designer: Paul Cherrill for Basement68
Picture research: Richard Spilsbury and Alice Harman
Proofreader and indexer: Martyn Oliver

Produced for Wayland by
White-Thomson Publishing Ltd
www.wtpub.co.uk

Wayland is a division of Hachette Children's Books,
an Hachette UK company.
www.hachette.co.uk

Picture Credits: 3 (right), Dreamstime/Sanclemenesdigpro; 6, Scie Photo Library/Dr Tony Brain and David Parker; 7 (top), Dreamstim Dmitry Kalinovsky; 7 (bottom), Shutterstock/Noah Strycker; 8 (top), Dreamstime/Joseph Gough; 8 (bottom), Dreamstime/Inga Nielsen; 9, Science Photo Library/Microfield Scientific Ltd; 10 (left Dreamstime/Michal Malysa; 10 (right), Dreamstime/Isselee; 11, Science Photo Library/Claude Nuridsany and Marie Perennou; 12, Dreamstime/Viacheslav Dyachkov; 13, Science Photo Library/Dav Scharf; 14, Shutterstock/Birute Vijeikiene; 15, Science Photo Librar Thomas Deerinck, NCMIR; 16, Shutterstock/D. Kucharski and K. Kucharska; 17, Science Photo Library/Power and Syred; 18, Wikime Commons/Gilles San Martin; 19, Science Photo Library/Dr Jeremy Burgess; 20, Dreamstime/Holger Leyrer; 21 (top), Science Photo Library/Power and Syred; 21 (bottom), Alamy/Robert Harding Pict Library Ltd; 22, Dreamstime/Marco Lijo; 23, Science Photo Library Steve Gschmeissner; 24 (left), Shutterstock/Gucio_55; 24 (right), Jolanta Dabrowska; 25, Science Photo Library/Steve Gschmeissne 26 (top), Shutterstock/EuToch; 26 (bottom), Shutterstock/Michael Pettigrew; 27 (top), Shutterstock/Robert Adrian Hillman; 27 (botto Science Photo Library/Dr Richard Kessel and Dr Gene Shih, Visual Unlimited; cover, Science Photo Library/Eye of Science.

CONTENTS

THE SCALE OF THINGS

At home we are never alone... The places we live in are ideal habitats for other living things. But many remain out of sight, or they are so small that we cannot see them without using powerful microscopes to zoom in on them. Then we can see these household horrors up close!

Bacteria are tiny living things that can coat almost every surface in a home. This is the tip of a pin (pink) coated with bacteria (orange).

Invisible world

It's hard to imagine how small some things really are. The smallest objects the human eye can see are about 0.2 mm long. There are 1000 **microns** to a millimeter. A human hair (with a width of about 100 microns) is vast, compared to most things scientists zoom in on!

Sense of scale

A scale tells you how big something is shown, compared to its real size. This is what it means when something is said to be 25 times its actual size. You'll see scales next to many images in this book, to give you a sense of the size of the objects.

These bacteria are **700 TIMES** their actual size

ools of the trade

ht **microscopes** use **lenses**—curved pieces glass—that bend light rays to magnify image (make it larger). They bounce light surfaces to create these images. The most werful microscopes can **magnify** things up about 2000 times. They can even make y bacteria visible.

ouse of horrors?

u'll see some weird and wonderful atures that share our houses in this book. ey might look rather horrific, but don't rry. Some are damaging or even harmful, t most are completely harmless.

A light microscope.

Humans are not the only sort of living thing that is found in our homes...

Scanning electron microscopes (SEMs)

These microscopes use electrons instead of light. (Electrons are tiny parts inside **atoms**.) SEMs bounce electrons off surfaces to create images. Electron microscopes can magnify things by almost a million times!

MOLDY OLD FOOD

You reach into the bread box to make a sandwich but—yuck—the loaf is covered with weird fuzzy green spots! What happened?

Mold attack

The bread is covered with **mold**. Mold is not a plant but a **fungus** (like mushrooms or toadstools). It grows by **digesting** plant or animal matter such as leaves, paper, dirt, and food. The mold on your bread isn't just on the surface. Its roots are like very thin threads and they spread inside food too. Time to find something else for lunch!

Mold breaks down dead and waste material and recycles it back into the soil.

Moldy cheese

We usually throw moldy food away, but so molds are safe and good to eat. Blue cheese such as Gorgonzola and Stilton, have greeni molds inside. Cheeses like Brie and Camem have white molds on the surface.

Stilton gets its tangy taste from the mold it contains.

...croscopic mushrooms?

...der a microscope, molds look like
...nny mushrooms! Bread mold has
...lks that grow up from its roots
...nich spread throughout the loaf),
...d spores at the ends of the
...lks. Molds release thousands
...these tiny spores into the air.
...e spores float away, and when
...y fall onto a piece of damp
...od, they grow into
...w molds.

This mould is **900 TIMES** its actual size

spores

stalk

KNOW YOUR FOE

Moldy food should be thrown away. People with asthma shouldn't smell or breathe molds. This is because molds can make them cough and sneeze and can cause itchy eyes and other problems.

It's the spores that give bread mold its greenish color.

Fearsome fact

Mold can cover a loaf of bread in less than three days!

9

NASTY HOUSEFLY HABITS

Houseflies look pretty harmless, don't they? Maybe so, but if you zoomed in on one it might make your stomach churn!

Dirty habits

Flies aren't fussy eaters. They will dine on dung heaps, rotting food, dead animals—anything that smells good to them. The problem is that, when they land on dirty things, the little hairs all over their body and legs pick up bacteria. Then, when they land on uncovered food, those bacteria rub off onto our dinner! That's not the worst bit. Flies produce feces (poo) every four or five minutes, usually while they are eating! Fly-swatter anyone?

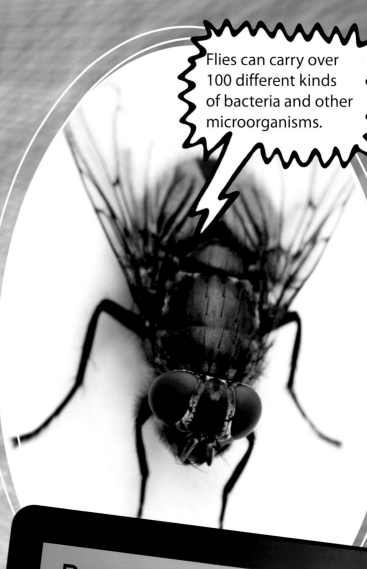

Flies can carry over 100 different kinds of bacteria and other microorganisms.

Most houseflies live within 3.2 km (2 miles) of where they were born, but will travel up to 32 km (20 miles) to find food!

Bye-bye fly

The easiest way to keep flies out of your home is to keep things clean. Don't leave food lying around, remove garbage regularly, and clean up messes right away, especially pet poo!

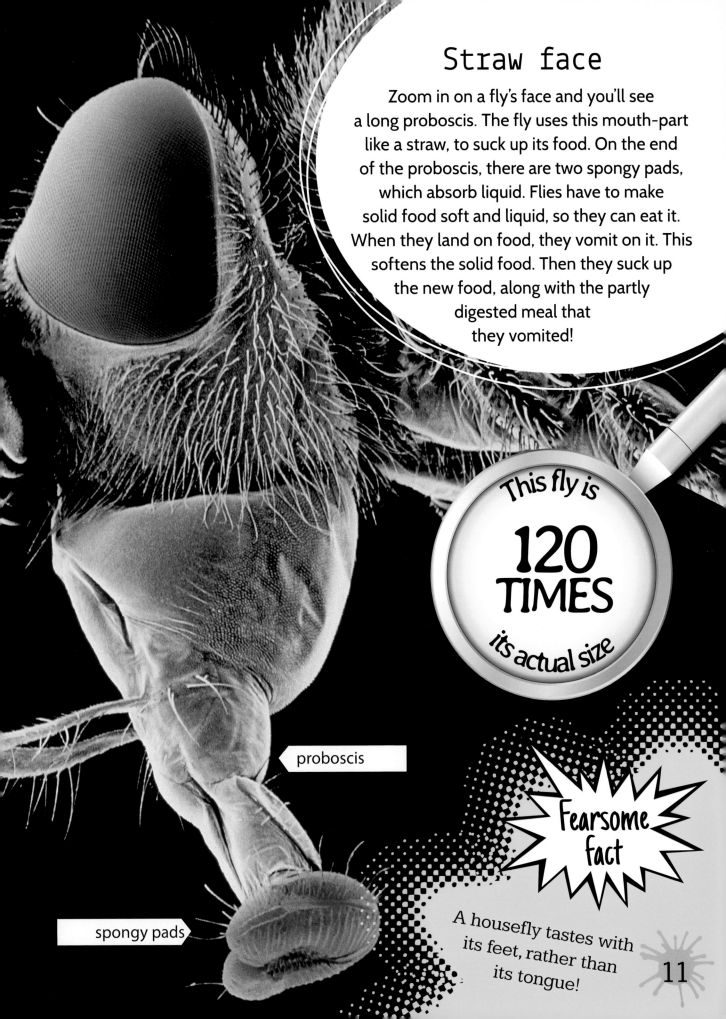

Straw face

Zoom in on a fly's face and you'll see a long proboscis. The fly uses this mouth-part like a straw, to suck up its food. On the end of the proboscis, there are two spongy pads, which absorb liquid. Flies have to make solid food soft and liquid, so they can eat it. When they land on food, they vomit on it. This softens the solid food. Then they suck up the new food, along with the partly digested meal that they vomited!

This fly is

120 TIMES

its actual size

proboscis

spongy pads

Fearsome fact

A housefly tastes with its feet, rather than its tongue!

CREEPY COCKROACHES

If you hear a hissing sound in the kitchen at night, it may be cockroaches. Shine a light at these flat, shiny beetles—and they will run away. They don't like light!

Contaminating cockroaches

Cockroaches rest during the day. Their flat bodies allow them to squeeze into the sm cracks in a kitchen. Then they come out at night to feed. Cockroaches eat almost anything they can find! When they eat ou food, they contaminate it with **saliva** (spit) and feces (poo). Cockroaches can be a pes because they can pass on nasty diseases caused by germs in their feces.

Perfect pets?

Only about 1 percent of the 3,500 differen kinds of cockroaches in the world are pest: Some people even keep cockroaches as pe

Cockroaches usually live near the kitchen so that they can find leftover food to eat.

KNOW YOUR FOE

You don't have to see a cockroach to know they are there. Cockroaches leave a trail of feces when they move around. The droppings look like tiny coffee beans. The smelly trails guide them to food in the dark.

skeleton

mouth-parts

antenna

This cockroach is **25 TIMES** its actual size

When a cockroach chews its food, its mouth-parts move from side to side, not up and down.

Close-up on cockroaches

When you zoom in on a cockroach, you will notice its **antennas**. These give the cockroach an excellent sense of smell. They sweep the air, searching for smells that help them to find food.

The skeleton on the outside of its body protects the cockroach. At the end of each leg it has a double claw and a footpad. These help the cockroach grip surfaces so it can move and climb quickly. It feels things through the hairs on its legs.

Related horrors

The Australian rhinoceros cockroach weighs up to 34 g (1.2 ounces) and is 8 cm (3 inches) long. This big beetle lives more than 10 years. Meanwhile, in Brazil there's a variety of cockroaches that are said to eat sleeping people's eyelashes!

Fearsome fact

Cockroaches can live three months without food and even survive explosions!

13

Shine a flashlight in the cellar or garage and you might spot something spinning from the roof. It is a cellar spider, disturbed by the light.

Gangly legs

The cellar spider has very long, skinny, gangly legs. It spins a messy web from silk produced in its cylinder-shaped body. The spider is a **predator** that uses its web to trap **prey**. It dangles upside down, with legs outstretched from its web. It shoots out its front legs to grab animals caught in its web.

Imagine having legs that are five times the length of your body! Cellar spiders are commonly known as daddy longlegs. (Crane flies are also known by this name.)

Cellar spiders prefer life out of the spotlight—in the dark, waiting for a meal.

KNOW YOUR FOE

Cellar spiders start spinning from their web when they are disturbed. They actually quiver back and forth on their legs. This means they look blurred to any possible predator, such as a larger spider, which may put off their attacker.

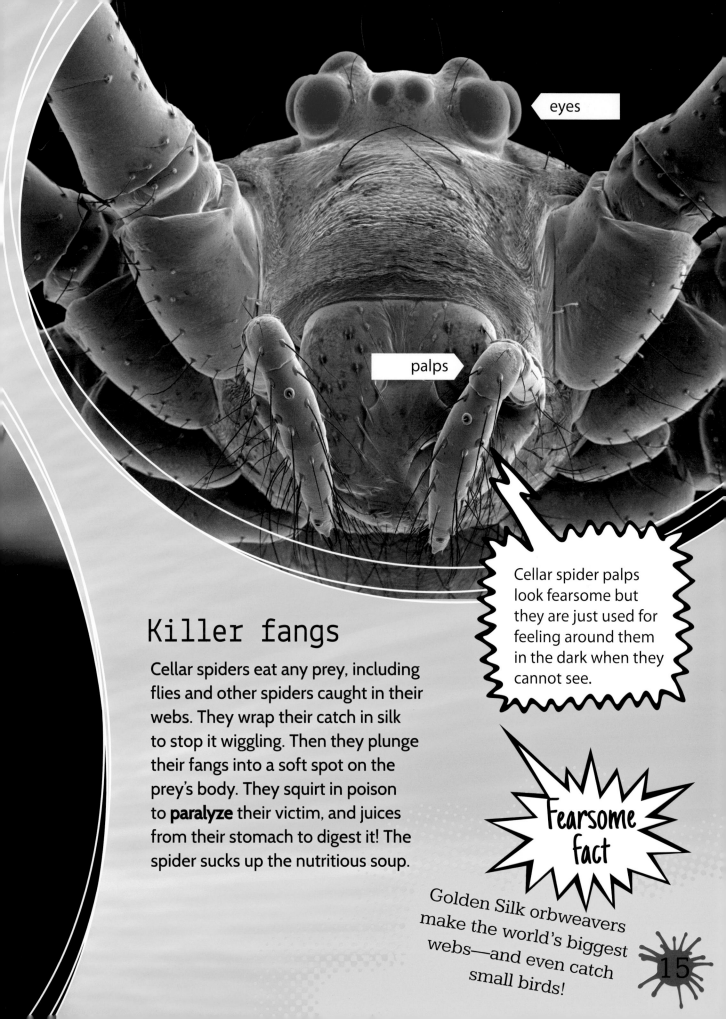

eyes

palps

Cellar spider palps look fearsome but they are just used for feeling around them in the dark when they cannot see.

Killer fangs

Cellar spiders eat any prey, including flies and other spiders caught in their webs. They wrap their catch in silk to stop it wiggling. Then they plunge their fangs into a soft spot on the prey's body. They squirt in poison to **paralyze** their victim, and juices from their stomach to digest it! The spider sucks up the nutritious soup.

Fearsome fact

Golden Silk orbweavers make the world's biggest webs—and even catch small birds!

CARPET CREATURES

Lie down on a carpet and you might imagine that you can hear a faint munching sound. Carpets are a favorite habitat and source of food for carpet beetle **larvae.**

Wooly bears!

Carpet beetles are black, as long as a grain of rice, and harmless. They feed on **nectar** and **pollen** from plants. But their tufty larvae—often called "wooly bears"—can cause lots of damage. They like nothing better than to feed on **keratin**. This is a na substance found, for example, in wool, feathers, and leather. If left undisturbed, wooly bears c ruin carpets and clothing

This is a carpet beetle larva, known as a wooly bear.

Museum beetles

Carpet beetles have small relatives called museum beetl These cause major damage in museums, for example by eating collections of rare drie butterflies, moths, and beetle

These larva hairs are **3000 TIMES** their actual size

Hairy weapons

Some people start scratching or even coughing when their homes have carpet beetles. Zoom in on the tiny hairs on the larva's back and you can see why. The hairs are shaped like spears that can stick to human skin, and they may cause rashes and other allergic reactions.

Trapped by smell

Pest controllers set traps containing **pheromone** chemicals that smell like male carpet beetles. Females attracted into the trap to mate with males are killed by **pesticides** there. Without females, there are no eggs and no damaging woolly bears.

Fearsome fact

Carpet beetles will also happily munch on seeds, nuts, and pet food!

SKIN-DEVOURING MITES

When you sink your head into your pillow every night, you might not be aware of all the activity inside it. Pillows, along with cushions and mattresses, can be home to thousands of tiny dust mites. Dust mites are short-legged relatives of spiders that feed on dead skin cells.

Skinny dust

Did you know that dead skin cells flake off from our bodies all the time? They are constantly replaced by new cells. The dead cells become part of household dust. The dust rains down all over our homes, but collects especially in pillows and mattresses. After all, we do spend one-third of our lives in bed!

Dust mites are so tiny they can blow into your house with dust.

east of the bed

oming in by at least 10x is the only way
see dust mites. They have eight legs, no
es, and long **chelicerae** (jaws) to chomp
cells. Dust mites like the warm, slightly
ist environment in pillows and mattresses.
hese conditions, dust mites
ed fast. A female can
up to 100 eggs
ring her
-week
span.

A dust mite, artificially colored green, feasts on skin cells.

This dust mite is **900 TIMES** its actual size

Other misbehaving mites

Several relatives of dust mites also live in or near homes, including flour mites, which live and feed in bags of flour. There are also straw itch mites, which can bite people handling straw or hay, leaving itchy red marks.

Fearsome fact

One-tenth of a typical pillow's weight is made up of dead dust mites and their droppings!

PAPER-MUNCHING SILVERFISH

Have the pages of some of your favorite books developed oddly shaped patches of paper, where the surface has been munched away? This is the work of the silverfish that live in dark, damp corners of many homes.

Glue for dinner!

Silverfish are flat, carrot-shaped insects without wings, around 1 cm (0.5 inches) lo... They use their large antennas to find their... around in the dark and to smell food. The... particularly enjoy eating wallpaper paste, the glue that is used to hold books togeth... as well as paper and photos.

KNOW YOUR FOE

Silverfish move fast. If you turn a light on in a dark room where they are feeding, they will quickly scurry into the shadows. They do this to stay out of sight of predators such as spiders and earwigs.

Silverfish are sleek and secretive insects.

These scales are **750 TIMES** their actual size

The scales on a silverfish are very delicate and powdery and form part of household dust in the houses where they live.

Scaley

...verfish are covered with ...ed, overlapping, silvery **scales**. ...ese look like fish scales up close, ...ich is how these creatures got their ...me. The scales help protect silverfish ... they squeeze into tight spaces ...d also prevent them from drying out. ...ey lose scales many times ...ring their eight-year lives. ...me people have an allergic ...ction when they breathe ...the tiny scales.

Going by many names

Silverfish go by different names—fishmoths, paramites, and carpet sharks. They have a very close relative, called a firebrat, that likes to live in warm places such as near ovens and fireplaces.

A silverfish, up close and personal!

Fearsome fact

A silverfish can survive a whole year without eating!

NASTY WASP NESTS

Wasp alert! Wasps live together in groups and build nests for their young. The trouble is that they often build nests in attics or other spaces in houses. A big nest can hold thousands and thousands of wasps, and they can sting people when they all leave the nest!

Paper houses

To make a nest, wasps scrape tiny bits of wood from trees, sheds, and fence posts with their powerful **mandibles** (jaws). They chew this up and mix it with saliva to produce a paste. Then they use the paste to build the walls, ledges, tunnels, and rooms of a nest.

Wasp warning

Bees sting only once but wasps can sting repeatedly. Wasp stings also give off a chemical that tells other wasps to attack, so don't swat a wasp near its nest or try to remove a wasp nest yourself. If you do, other wasps will join in the attack!

A wasp's nest has many little compartments where eggs can develop into adult wasps.

This wasp's mouth is **100 TIMES** its actual size

mandibles

This colored SEM image shows a wasp's spongy tongue in red.

tongue

asp mouth
t work

om in on a wasp's mouth and you'll
e something surprising! Wasps don't have
traw-shaped mouth like bees. Instead they
ve a short, bumpy tongue. They use this
lick up liquids like nectar and the juices
ripe fruit. Close up, you can also see the
werful mandibles that wasps use for
bbing, chopping, and cutting things.

Fearsome fact

A wasp nest can contain 3000–5000 wasps and be as large as a beach ball!

WIGGLY WOODWORMS

Your home may be under attack! Are your chairs, tables, or floors being eaten by woodworms? Look for tiny holes in wooden furniture or floorboards, and piles of wood dust next to them. These are the signs that woodworms are present.

Hungry woodworms can damage and weaken furniture.

Tunneling terrors

Woodworms aren't worms at all. They are th larvae of the furniture beetle. Female furnitu beetles lay their eggs in cracks in the wood. When long, wiggly larvae hatch out of the e; they start to eat their way down into the wo They eat and eat until they are big enough t turn into adult beetles. Then they eat their w out of the wood. The adults fly off to lay mc eggs that produce more greedy woodworm:

Adults that emerge from the wood are small, oval, brown beetles about 4–6 mm long.

KNOW YOUR FOE

When a woodworm larva transforms into an adult, it makes a little round exit hole in the wood. The adults don't feed; they only live long enough to reproduce!

This woodworm larva is **120 TIMES** its actual size

A woodworm can live inside wood for up to four years.

mouth-parts

legs

Lousy larva

When you look at a woodworm up close, you can see it has three pairs of very small legs at the top of its body. It uses these to drag itself through its tunnels. It releases a special substance from its mouth-parts that helps to make wood soft and easier to eat.

Fearsome fact

Adult furniture beetles leave holes 2 mm across when they leave the wood. Longhorn beetle larvae leave holes five times wider!

TERMITE INVADERS

In some parts of the world, the most destructive pests are tiny and work in teams. Carpenter termites tunnel into the basements of homes to find wood to eat. If no one stops them, termites can demolish whole buildings!

Living together

Carpenter termites are insects that live in groups or **colonies**. There may be as many as 2 million termites in one colony! Most termites in a colony are workers. They build underground nests for the colony and search for wood to eat. They share the wood with the **queen**, who lays eggs in the nest, and other termites who look after the young and defend the colony from attackers.

A mud tube keeps termites moist and hidden from predators as they g in and out of a house.

Blind worker termites find food by following smell trails.

26

ood shredders

penter termites have white, soft bodies,
hard, jagged mandibles. They use these
ndibles to saw off tiny pieces of wood the
e of a grain of sand. When they chomp away
wood that supports a house, it can collapse!

nternal colony

mites can only eat wood because of the
n tinier animals that live in their stomachs.
ese digest the wood and release **nutrients** for
termites, in return for a safe place to live.

Timber! Termites can gradually destroy houses if they are not spotted soon enough.

Soldier termites have the biggest mandibles of all termites. They use these weapons to defend the colony.

Fearsome fact

Working together, a colony of termites can remove 400 g (13 ounces) of wood a day!

Glossary

allergic reaction–when someone is badly affected by eating, touching, or breathing in a substance, such as household dust or nuts

antennas–pair of feelers on an insect's head that they use to feel and taste

asthma–breathing difficulties resulting from an allergy

atom–smallest unit of a chemical that can take part in a chemical reaction

bacteria–simple, tiny living things that live in air, water, soil, and within other living things

cell–the smallest, most basic unit, from which all living things are made

chelicerae–pointed mouth-parts of spiders and their relatives

colony–group of animals that live together in the same place

digest–break down food into small pieces that the body can absorb and use

fungus–type of plant (such as mold) that usually grows on other plants or on rotting material

habitat–area or environment where something (such as a plant or animal) lives

keratin–type of tough protein that forms animal tissues such as skin, hair, nails, and feathers

larva–young that hatch from eggs of certain types of animals including insects, fish, and frogs

lens–curved piece of glass that bends light rays; used in microscopes and magnifying glasses

magnify–make bigger; enlarge

mandible–hard, cutting or crushing mouth-parts

micron–unit of measurement equal to one-millionth of a meter; 50 microns is about half the width of a human hair

microscope–device that produces enlarged images of objects that are normally too small to be seen

mold–type of soft fungus that usually grows on damp surfaces

nectar–sweet liquid made by plants to attract insects and other animals to spread their pollen

palp–type of jointed soft mouth-part in animals (including insects and crabs)

paralyze–make something unable to feel or move part or all of its body

pesticide–chemical used to kill insects and other animals that are pests

pollen–fine powder that forms in flowers and is carried to other flowers by insects

predator–animal that hunts and eats other animals

prey–animal that is hunted and eaten by other animals

proboscis–tube-shaped mouth-part used for sucking up fluids such as nectar or blood

queen–in insects such as ants, termites, and bees, the queen is the largest individual in the group, which produces eggs

scales–thin, overlapping plates covering the skin of many fish, reptiles and some insects